radar

body decoration

Adam Sutherland

Published in 2013 by Wayland

Copyright © Wayland 2013

Wayland
Hachette Children's Books
338 Euston Road
London NW1 3BH

Wayland Australia
Level 17/207 Kent Street
Sydney NSW 2000

All rights reserved

Concept by Joyce Bentley

Commissioned by Debbie Foy and Rasha Elsaeed

Produced for Wayland by Calcium
Designer: Paul Myerscough
Editor: Sarah Eason

Photographer: Meg Hawkins

British Library Cataloguing in Publication Data

Body decoration. — (Art on the street)(Radar)
 1. Body art—Juvenile literature.
 I. Series
 709'.040752-dc22

ISBN: 978 0 7502 7789 1

Every effort has been made to clear copyright. Should there be any inadvertent omission, please apply to the publisher for rectification.

10 9 8 7 6 5 4 3 2 1

Printed in China

Wayland is a division of Hachette Children's Books, an Hachette UK company.

www.hachette.co.uk

Acknowledgements: Corbis: Reuters 14l; iStockphoto: Luca Cepparo cover; RexFeatures: F1 Online 15l, Sipa Press 26; Shutterstock: 1171 30bl, Kharidehal Abhirama Ashwin 7br, AISPIX 28tr, Andrey Arkusha 28br, Lucian Coman 28cl, Kobby Dagan 13, Lev Dolgachov 29tl, Olga Ekaterincheva 9cr, Helga Esteb 2b, 16, Icons Jewelry 2–3, Iofoto 23br, Elena Itsenko 11br, Nicky Jacobs 8tr, Donald Joski 9t, Andy Lim 20–21, Vasilchenko Nikita 11bc, Ostill 23tr, Dmitriy Pochitalin 1, PZAxe 11bl, Omer N Raja 14r, Pavel Reband 15r, Rsfatt 22cl, Alexey Stiop 4–5, StockHouse 22br, Mikhail Tchkheidze 9bl, Timur G 3br, Dusaleev Viatcheslav 31tr, VSO 27tr, Vladimir Wrangel 12;

cover stories

the**people**

the**art**

the**talk**

BODIES INC.

Body decoration takes place in all cultures. From pierced ears to nail art or colourful tattoos, millions of people decorate their bodies to enhance their look or show their connection to a group or subculture.

Earrings and beyond!

Ear piercing is the most common form of body piercing, with lips, noses and tongues following close behind. Others go beyond piercing and stretch their earlobes for a more dramatic look.

Hair flair

Many cultures have altered or enhanced their hair in dramatic ways. Today, many people lengthen their hair with extensions or weaves, grow it into thick dreadlocks, or use hair dye and styling gels.

Colourful nail art

Many people wear colourful designs on their fingernails and toenails, and a worldwide industry of nail bars has appeared to fulfil this demand.

Skin deep

The practice of tattooing grew out of traditional African and American tribal markings. Today, tattooing is big business. There are even television shows dedicated to tattoo artists and their clients!

Paint power

Cosmetic make-up has always been the most widely used form of body decoration. Face and body painting used to be done with clay, charcoal or henna, but modern-day artists create amazing, colourful designs with specially formulated paints.

ANCIENT MARKINGS

Maori people tattooed their bodies to show their status within a tribe. The tattoos of this sixteenth century Maori chief display his importance.

Body decoration has been around almost as long as the human race. Historians believe that tattooing goes back at least 10,000 years, and piercing 4,000 years. Tribes in the Far East and across Northern Europe had their own preferred markings, depending on their superstitions or how they were 'ranked' in society.

Oldest ink

The oldest recorded tattoos belong to 'Ötzi the Iceman', who died around 3,300 BCE. His preserved body was found in the Austrian Alps in 1991. Some of his 57 tattoos are believed to be for tribal or religious purposes, others are thought to have been for the treatment of arthritis! Tattooed 2,500-year-old Egyptian mummies have also been discovered.

Ear ornaments

The oldest earrings date back to 2,500 BCE and were found in a grave in Iraq. Metal earrings were originally thought to prevent spirits entering the body through the ears. Later, earrings became a symbol of wealth – ancient Romans wore precious stones in their ears, and the ancient Egyptians wore expensive gold hoops.

Polynesian 'tatao'

The word 'tatao' was brought to the West by British explorer Captain Cook, who travelled to the Polynesian island Tahiti twice between 1768–1775. There, he met tribesmen covered with traditional markings. Their skin was cut with sharp bone chisels. These were then dipped in 'ink' (which was was often made from burnt caterpillars) and tapped into the skin.

Rings and studs

Ear piercing was thought to have been practised by Eskimos on the Arctic Circle around 3500 BCE as a sign of status. Nose piercing was first recorded in Iraq and Iran 4,000 years ago, and was brought to Europe and the USA in the 1960s by Western travellers returning from India. Tongue piercing was originally performed by the Aztecs to draw blood for the gods.

Stained skin

Henna comes from a plant that grows naturally across the Middle East and Indian subcontinent. It has been used as a body decoration for more than 5,000 years. The plant can be ground into a paste and left on skin to temporarily stain it. Henna was believed to bring luck, and is still used in many parts of the world in festivals and celebrations. It is traditionally worn by Indian brides to decorate their hands, palms and fingernails.

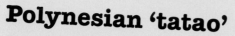

Henna tattooing is called 'mehndi' in India, where it is an age-old tradition.

7

SKIN-TASTIC!

Many people love altering their appearance. Some do it permanently, others prefer something temporary. Here are some of the most popular methods.

Ink for life

Tattooing is usually done with an electric tattoo machine. The machine pushes needles into the skin between 50 and 3,000 times a minute. The needles penetrate the skin by about one millimetre, depositing a drop of insoluble ink with each puncture into the layer of skin called the dermis. The ink stays in place for a person's whole life. Tattoo artists should always use sterile, disposable needles to avoid infection.

Part-time tattoos

Harquus is a temporary paint that looks just like a tattoo. It is water resistant, and does not penetrate or dye the skin. It can last for a few days.

Put a ring in it

Piercing is when a hole is made in the skin so that a stud, ring or other type of jewellery can be worn. The hole is often made with a 'piercing gun'. Ear piercing was started by tribes in South America and Africa as a way to protect against evil spirits thought to enter the body via the ears!

The hole truth

Stretching is the expansion of a healed piercing, usually in the ear. A 'taper' is often used – a rod that gets thicker at one end. In ancient times, stretched ears were a symbol of wealth. Rich merchants collected gold, which they melted down and turned into earrings. Gold is a heavy metal, so it stretched the ears. The longer their ears, the richer the merchants appeared!

harquus

ink tattoos

piercing

stretching

Type 'harquus demonstration' into www.youtube.com to see how this body decoration is created.

ORLA ZUSMAN

Orla, 18, works as a nail artist for the UK chain Nails Inc. Here, she tells Radar readers why she loves her job.

Why did you choose nails as a career?

I've always loved art, and I love to express myself! I also enjoy meeting new people. Every day is different. It's a challenge creating new styles and designs for each person.

What makes a good nail artist?

You need to be creative, and you also need to have a strong opinion. Clients will often come in and not know how they want their nails to look, so it's my job to talk to them, find out more about them, and suggest ideas that I think match their personality. Some people want to follow the latest trends, others prefer more classic, timeless designs.

What did you learn at college?

We were taught the science of nails – how they grow and how diet can affect them. We then practised shaping the nails, and moved on to painting and decorating them. We started learning with dark colours. They are harder to apply, because the nail varnish is thicker and if you make a mistake, it's more obvious!

Why do you think nail art is so popular now?

Firstly, nail art is relatively inexpensive. Secondly, it's not permanent – you can change your design to match your outfit! Lastly, I would say that because nail bars are so common, it is also much more accessible.

How long is your working day?

I usually do six- or eight-hour shifts, but I often get carried away on a client's design and end up staying longer.

Why do you think people like such eye-catching designs?

I think it's great to feel special, or unique, particularly for an important occasion. One of my customers came in for a design for her daughter's wedding day. She chose a circle of crystals on her own ring finger to commemorate the day.

What are the most common nail designs you are asked for?

Crystals are very popular – we add tiny gems to the nails to create amazing designs. We also get asked to create initials, half-moon shapes and glitter work. Recently, a lot of people have been asking for animal print designs. We use different colours to apply zebra or leopard prints to the nails.

11

PAINTED FACES

Make-up isn't a modern invention. In fact, cosmetics – particularly lipstick, eyeliner and foundation – were used by the ancient Egyptians as far back as 4,000 BCE. Some early cosmetics were made from crushed plants and other harmless substances, but others contained poisons that had harmful effects on the wearer!

This bust of the ancient Egyptian queen Nefertiti shows her eyes heavily lined with kohl.

Ancient eyes

Ancient Egyptians outlined their eyes with a substance called kohl, made from a mixture of lead, copper, burned almonds, soot and other ingredients. They believed that eye make-up could improve eyesight and ward off evil spirits. In Rome, cosmetics were usually made by special female slaves called Cosmetae.

Early nail polish

The Chinese began to stain their fingernails with a mixture of gelatin, beeswax and egg from around 3,000 BCE. They used different colours depending on their social class – Chou dynasty royals wore gold and silver; later royals wore black or red. The lower classes were forbidden from wearing 'royal' colours.

Geisha make-up

In Japan, traditional female entertainers called geisha coloured their faces and necks white using rice powder. They sometimes mixed it with bird droppings for a lighter colour! They then painted their eyebrows, lips and eyelids with a paste made from crushed flower petals.

Victorian ladies

Nineteenth century ladies also preferred pale skin. Make-up was rarely used, although cheeks were sometimes reddened with rouge, a coloured powder made from beetroot. Fine blue lines were often painted on the skin to increase the appearance of delicate skin with veins showing through!

Along with their distinctive make-up, geisha also wore elaborate hair decorations, including decorative combs and fabric flowers.

Perfect pale skin

Between the fourteenth and seventeenth centuries, the European lower classes often worked on the land, and so their skin became tanned by the sun. For the upper classes therefore, pale skin became a sign of wealth and social status. Both men and women artificially lightened their skin. White lead paint was one of the methods they used. It contained a poison called arsenic, which killed many of its users. In spite of its dangers, Queen Elizabeth I regularly applied white lead to her face!

Make-up today

In the early twentieth century, make-up became fashionable in the USA and Europe thanks to ballet, theatre and, most importantly, the new Hollywood film industry. Mass-market cosmetics companies were founded by Max Factor, Elizabeth Arden, L'Oréal and Helena Rubinstein – names that are still popular on the high street today.

GOING GLOBAL

Amazing body decoration, from neck rings to face painting, exists around the world. Here are some of the most eye-catching examples.

South America

The Kayapo people live in the Amazon rainforest in South America. They mark their faces and bodies with tattoos that they believe guard against evil 'spirits' thought to live in the forest. Some Kayapo men also insert disks into their lower lips to stretch the skin.

India

Indian weddings are very colourful events that last for several days. The bride wears outfits in colours thought to bring good luck,

Today, only older Kayapo men (top left) still stretch their bottom lip. An Indian bride's jewellery was once part of her dowry – money given to her husband as part of the wedding arrangements.

especially red. She may also have henna patterns on her hands, forearms, legs and feet, and may wear ornate earrings and forehead decorations called bindi.

New Zealand

Maori warriors used to scar and tattoo their faces with bone chisels to frighten their enemies. Today, the less permanent

Tattooed Maori warriors (left) pull faces to add to their fearsome appearance. Painting the body (top) is an art form in its own right.

tradition of face painting carries the same meanings of power and authority within a tribe as the original form.

Austria

In 1998, Austria hosted the first World Bodypainting Festival. The event has since grown to become the biggest festival of its kind with more than 200 artists and 30,000 visitors attending.

England

The London Tattoo Convention has been running since 2005. It attracts more than 20,000 visitors from around the world, as well as famous tattoo artists, such as Robert Hernandez and Roberto Borsi.

United States

The San Francisco Tattoo Museum covers the history of tattooing in the USA. Run by well-known tattooist Lyle Tuttle, it houses antique tattoo guns, portraits of famous subjects and sheets of historical tattoo artwork.

15

KAT VON D

THE STATS

Name: Katherine von Drachenberg
Born: 8 March 1982
Place of birth: Monterrey, Nuevo Leon, Mexico
Job: Tattoo artist, TV star

Among countless other tattoos, Kat has a 'sleeve' design on both arms.

The star of tattoo TV

Career highlights

1996 did her first tattoo on a friend

2008 founded the MusInk Tattoo Convention and Music Festival

2010 opened the Wonderland Gallery, an art gallery and boutique shop, next door to her tattoo parlour

2010 Kat's second book, *The Tattoo Chronicles*, is published and reached Number 3 on *The New York Times* Bestseller List

Growing up

Kat was born in Mexico, but moved to the USA with her family when she was just four years old. Growing up, Kat was always sketching pictures and designs. In her teens, she told her parents that she wanted to be a doctor like her father, but he was convinced that Kat had a natural skill for drawing, and encouraged her to pursue her talent and make a living out of art instead.

Tattoo culture

As a teenager, Kat was inspired by rock and punk music, and the fashion and lifestyle that went with them. She got her first tattoo, a 'J' on her ankle, while still in her teens and working in a tattoo parlour, Sin City in San Bernardino, California. It was here that the customers christened her Kat von D. Her love of music has led to Kat having tattoos of her favourite bands, including Guns 'N' Roses, AC/DC and ZZ Top.

Getting a break on TV

Kat eventually found a job as a tattoo artist in a shop in Hollywood, where she met the tattoo artist Chris Garver.

Chris left the shop to star in *Miami Ink*, a TV reality show about the everyday lives of tattoo artists and their customers. Six months later he asked Kat to join him. She was the only woman on the show and a talented tattooist, but more importantly, she had a talent for getting close to customers, understanding completely what they wanted, and how much their tattoos meant to them. She was such a hit with viewers that Kat was offered her own show in Los Angeles.

Superstar status

LA Ink, set in Kat's High Voltage tattoo parlour, has turned her into a celebrity. The show has been running since 2007 and is a big hit, watched by more than three million people. Kat has tattooed famous names including *Lost* actor Dominic Monaghan, and Steve-O and Bam Margera from the hit MTV show *Jackass*. She launched a range of make-up for beauty store Sephora, and her first two books reached *The New York Times* Bestseller list. She recently released her third book, *Go Big or Go Home,* in 2013. Maybe sometimes parents really do know best!

MAKE EARRINGS!

Want to add something fun and eye-catching to your outfit for a special occasion? All you need is a few items from a craft store!

You will need:

- 2 metal earring hooks
- 2 pieces of jewellery wire with a looped end
- round-nosed pliers
- assorted beads

1 Thread a bead onto the end of your jewellery wire.

2 Use your pliers to curl the straight end of the jewellery wire into a double 'knot'.

3 Use your pliers to pull open the looped end of your earring hook.

4

Hook the loop of the jewellery wire onto the 'opened' loop of the earring hook.

Type 'make earrings' into www.youtube.com to see some great ideas.

5

Use your pliers to squeeze the loop of the earring hook closed again. Congratulations, you have made your first earring! Repeat steps 1 to 5 to make the second earring.

Got it?

Experiment with different colours, numbers and sizes of beads. If you find using the pliers difficult at first, ask an adult to help you with steps 2 and 3 then try to complete 4 and 5 on your own.

AMAZING BODIES!

Check out the surprising – and sometimes painful – ways some people have ended up in the record books.

LONGEST SESSION

Who: Dave Fleet and James Llewellyn
When: 2011
Where: Cardiff Bay, UK
What: Longest tattoo session
How: Fleet spent 50 hours and 10 minutes tattooing biblical scenes onto James Llewellyn's body, raising £2,300 for Cancer Research Wales.

MOST TATTOOED MAN

Who: Lucky Diamond Rich
When: Since 2006
Where: Sydney, Australia
What: World's most tattooed person
How: Street entertainer Lucky has spent thousands of hours in the tattooist's chair. One hundred per cent of his body is covered in black ink, including his eyelids and even his gums! He has now started having white designs tattooed on top of the black.

HAIR RAISING!

Who: Kazuhiro Watanabe
When: 2013
Where: Japan
What: World's tallest mohican
How: Kazuhiro's mohican is a massive 113 centimetres, which took him 15 years to grow!

TWILIGHT TATTOO!

Who: Cathy Ward
When: 2011
Where: Reading, UK
What: World's largest *Twilight* tattoo
How: Cathy's love of the *Twilight* books and films prompted her to spend 22 hours under the needle to create a likeness of Robert Pattinson and his friends that covers her whole back!

MOST PIERCED WOMAN

Who: Elaine Davidson
When: Since 2000
Where: Edinburgh, Scotland
What: World's most pierced woman
How: When Elaine became a record breaker back in 2000, she had 462 piercings, including 192 on her face! Since then, the number has grown to nearly 7,000, weighing over 3kg!

EXPENSIVE NAILS

Who: Azature
When: 2012
Where: Hollywood, USA
What: World's most expensive nail polish
How: Famed for their luxurious fine jewellery, Azature created an exclusive Black Diamond nail polish which sells for £160,000! It contains 267 carats of black diamonds, and 60 hand-set black diamonds in the lid!

COOL OR FOOL?

Body decoration divides public opinion. Supporters say that it is a positive expression of individuality. They believe that:

1. It is all about freedom of expression. People should be free to adorn their own body in whatever way they want.
2. To condemn body decoration is to condemn thousands of years of tradition and beliefs in many cultures around the world.
3. Tattooing is an art form in its own right. Many tattoo artists are respected for their work, in the same way as more traditional artists. Tattoo designs have made their way into fashion and art galleries.
4. Some forms of body decoration are non-invasive and temporary and so are no different from putting on make-up.
5. Extreme hairstyles, piercings or tattoos can indicate membership of a social group. They can help people to feel part of a subculture, and give them a sense of purpose and belonging.
6. Children as young as three are often encouraged to wear face paint or have temporary tattoos. Why should it be so different for teenagers or adults?

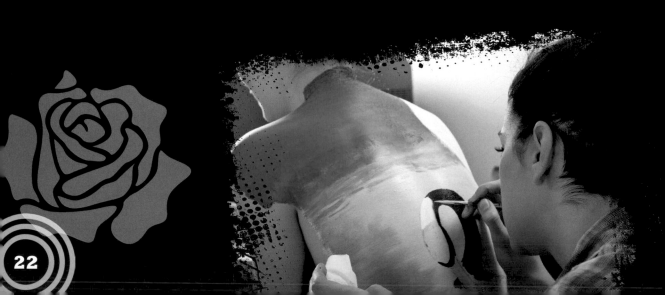

Some people are strongly opposed to others adorning their bodies and changing their appearance. They say:

1. Piercings, tattoos and extreme hairstyles can appear to be antisocial or even threatening.
2. Piercings can be dangerous. They can get caught, ripped out or even become infected. Some people have died after multiple body piercings.
3. If tattoos are not expertly done using sterile needles, they can become infected. People have been known to contract diseases, such as hepatitis, from this art form.
4. A tattoo is meant to be permanent. If a person decides they no longer like it, it is an expensive and painful process to have it removed. Once removed, the skin is still scarred.
5. Permanent types of body decoration can seem like a good idea when you are young. Years later they may look inappropriate or strange.

AGAINST

RIGHT OR WRONG?

Body decoration is an ancient tradition that is still respected in many cultures. However, it can look threatening and can be off-putting to certain sections of society. As a result, people with lots of tattoos and piercings can find it hard to be accepted. Body decoration is not for everyone, but in many societies people are allowed to express themselves freely, as long as they are not harming others.

NAIL FLOWERS

Nail art is a fun and easy way to turn your hands into temporary works of art!

You will need:

- base coat varnish
- 2 colours of nail varnish
- hairpin
- clear nail varnish

1 On clean, dry hands, paint a clear base coat. Let this dry out completely.

2 Paint your chosen background colour. Let this dry out completely. If it is still wet when you follow with the later steps, it will smear.

3 Make a dot in the middle of each nail with your second varnish colour.

4

Now use the hairpin to put five small dots of varnish around the dot in the centre of each nail. This will make a flower pattern. Let the varnish dry out completely.

5

When the flower is completely dry, paint your nails with clear nail varnish.

Got it?

Once you have mastered the basic nail flower, be adventurous and try different coloured flowers on each nail, or even flowers with five different coloured petals!

Type 'nail art designs' into www.youtube.com to see some fun nail art.

Type 'Ed Hardy T-shirts' into www.youtube.com to see some of his stunning designs.

Actress Ling Bai added tattoo cool to her style when she wore an Ed Hardy jacket to a *Star Magazine* party.

TATTOOS MEAN BUSINESS

In the last 50 years, tattooing has gone from the underground to the mainstream. Designs by tattooists such as Ed Hardy and Sailor Jerry are being used to sell playing cards, clothes and shoes! Today, tattooing is big business.

Starting the trend

Ed Hardy is one of the world's highest profile tattooists. Born in California in 1945, Ed was a gifted artist, and studied for a degree in printmaking before deciding to follow his first love: tattooing.

Ed's mix of traditional Eastern and Western characters quickly made him a familiar name in the tattoo community, but thanks to a business partnership with French marketing expert Christian Audigier, people around the world have become fans of Ed's colourful designs.

Since 2004, Ed's artwork has been used on everything from T-shirts and baseball caps to trainers. Not only is his business worth US$20 million (£12.3 million) a year, but collectors are also queuing up to buy his original prints for their walls.

Fellow tattoo artist

Ed's teacher was a tattooist called Sailor Jerry. Born Norman Keith Collins in Nevada in 1911, he joined the US Navy at 19 and travelled the world. Sailor Jerry's tattoo skills were heavily influenced by the same areas of the Pacific that Captain Cook (see page 7) visited. His groundbreaking designs proved very popular back in the USA and are now also being used to sell products. Trainer brand Converse used Jerry's images for a range of hi-top shoes, and his designs also appear on bottles of Sailor Jerry spiced rum. Jerry died in 1973, but his artwork has been collected together in books that sell for between US $300 and US $400 (£185 and £250).

Worldwide profits

By successfully using the rebellious imagery of tattoo artists to sell products, companies have made tattooing more noticeable. Today, more than 45 million Americans have at least one tattoo. The ones that don't, probably own an Ed Hardy T-shirt!

27

HAIR- RAISING STYLES

skinhead

cornrows

mohican

dreadlocks

Body decoration goes beyond the skin. A distinctive hairstyle is one obvious way to show imagination, originality, creativity and self expression. Here are some of the most well-known and popular styles.

Simply shaved

The skinhead 'hairstyle', with hair cut extremely short or even shaved off completely, started in the UK in the 1960s, and soon spread to other parts of the world. Both men and women wore the style. Although the skinhead later became associated with aggression and racism, the original skinheads were not politically motivated or violent.

Complicated cornrows

This is a traditional West African style where the hair is braided very close to the scalp. The style was brought to the USA by slaves and worn by both men and women. It regained popularity in the 1960s and 1970s as part of the 'Black Power' movement, and is now popular once again with the spread of hip-hop culture.

Amazing mohican

This dramatic hairstyle – with the centre of the hair long and spiked, and the sides often shaved – is usually associated with the Mohawk tribe of Native Americans. Punks adopted the mohican in the 1970s, often dying their hair bright colours and shaping it into 'liberty spikes' to resemble the Statue of Liberty, in New York, USA.

No brush necessary

Dreadlocks are matted strands of hair, often associated with the Rastafarian religion that originated in Jamaica in the West Indies. They are usually intentionally formed by backcombing the hair and not brushing it. The hair tangles as it grows, and forms long, twisted strands that look like rope.

BODY TALK

Decorate your vocabulary with our Radar guide!

afro
a thick and curly hair style with a rounded shape

beehive
a hairstyle in which the front of the hair is backcombed so that it sits high on the head

black henna
an illegal tattoo ink made from black hair dye. It can result in severe allergic reaction

bob
a hairstyle in which the hair is cut to jaw-length and the ends are curled under or flicked out

body modification
altering or changing the body with tattoos and/or piercings

body painting
decorating the body with paint specially formulated for use on the skin

body 'suit'
when the entire body, including the head, is tattooed

facial ornamentation
facial piercings

French manicure
a manicure in which the nails are painted in a pale pink or beige colour and the tips of the nails are painted white

henna
a reddish dye made from the powdered leaves of a plant

Irezumi tattoo
a tattoo that is done by hand and which traditionally comes from Japan

labret
any small object inserted into the lip as an ornament

mohican
a hairstyle in which the sides of the head are often shaved, while the centre is grown long and styled into a stiff shape

pedicure
a treatment in which the skin of the feet is smoothed and the toenails are shaped and polished

pigment
a substance found in plants or animals that creates a certain colour. A good example of this is food colouring

sleeve
when a person's arm is tattooed from the wrist to the shoulder

tattoo gun
an electric machine used for tattooing

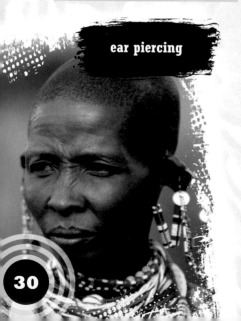
ear piercing

GLOSSARY

body painting

arthritis
a painful condition in which the joints of the body swell

commemorate
an act carried out in order to remember something or someone

condemn
to strongly disapprove of something

convention
a large meeting of a group with shared interests

dermis
the deep inner layer of the skin, containing blood vessels

distinctive
something that is eye-catching, or instantly recognisable

hepatitis
a condition in which the liver becomes inflamed

insoluble
incapable of being dissolved

mainstream
a part of popular culture

merchant
a person involved in the buying and selling of goods, or merchandise, for profit. Merchants used to trade gold, spices and slaves

Mohawk tribe
a Native American tribe that took its name from the Mohawk Valley in upstate New York

non-invasive
without piercing the skin or leaving permanent marks

penetrate
to pierce, enter or push through something

Polynesia
a group of islands in the Pacific Ocean

Rastafarian
a member of a Jamaican 'religion' that regards the former emperor of Ethiopia, Haile Selassie (also known as Ras Tafari) as God

sterile
free from bacteria

subculture
a small part of mainstream culture, with its own attitudes, beliefs and influences

underground
hidden or secret; not well known to many people

AMAZING ART!

Dig into the past

Body decoration has a fascinating past. The more you read, the more you will appreciate all the thousands of years of history and beliefs that have gone into the tattoos, piercings, make-up designs and even hairstyles of people you see in the street. For some background reading on hairstyles throughout the decades look at:
www.hairarchives.com
Check out Kat von D's website to see some of her amazing tattoo designs:
www.katvond.net
See how tattoo design has crossed over into fashion on Ed Hardy's website:
www.edhardyshop.com

Reads & Apps

There are lots of great books on body decoration. Here are Radar's favourites:

Be Beautiful: Every Girl's Guide to Hair, Skin and Make-up by Alice Hart-Davis and Molly Hindhaugh (Walker, 2009)

Cozy's Complete Guide to Girls' Hair by Cozy Friedman (Workman, 2011)

Get the fashion without the pain! The *iPierce* app allows you to place various piercings onto photos of yourself! For nail fun try *Dress Up and Makeup: Manicure*. Download both apps from:
www.itunes.com

INDEX